CONTENTS

I INTRODUCTION

Current developments in the reform of local government place partnership working centre stage. Best value, designed to get local authorities to adopt new ways of delivering services in order to secure continuous improvement in service delivery, actively encourages the use of partnerships. The new power of well-being, that enables local authorities to promote the economic, social and environmental well-being of the community, is also designed to facilitate partnership working.

The draft guidance on the power of well-being published by the DETR in December 2000 states "the well-being provisions not only confer new powers on councils to achieve a certain *end* (the promotion of well-being), they also expand the range of *means* available to councils to pursue that end. So, in pursuit of well-being, councils are able to establish companies and other forms of corporate body, to create pooled budgets, to undertake lead or joint commissioning, and to integrate the provision of their services with those of other service providers" (paragraph 45 of the draft guidance). This relates to another key government objective where partnership working plays a key role - that of providing 'joined-up government' with public services as a whole being better co-ordinated.

When a council is considering partnership working for a particular activity it will need to choose an appropriate structure from a wide range of options that are available. There are key considerations for each option and the decision on the choice of vehicle will very much depend on the local concerns and priorities identified by the council.

Although this report provides information on the different types of partnership structures that are available (chapter 6) the focus is on local authority involvement in companies. This is for three main reasons. The first relates to the complex nature of the company model. The role of a local authority company can range from that of an agent, performing different types of co-ordinating functions between different partners, to that of a completely free-standing and independent entity engaged in trading and other commercial activities. The purpose for which a company is established can also vary greatly. Companies can be established for not-for-profit purposes in the form of Industrial and Provident Societies or companies limited by guarantee or they can be registered as charities. Alternatively they can be used where getting a good return on investment is one of the main objectives. Companies established for trading and other commercial purposes are generally set up as companies limited by shares.

Added to this is the fact that the degree of local authority involvement in the company can also vary greatly. At one end of the spectrum is the company that is wholly owned and/or controlled by the local authority that established it, to the other end of the spectrum where the company is owned and controlled by other organisations with the local authority being a minority shareholder controlling less than 20 per cent of the voting rights in the company.

The second reason for focusing on companies in this report relates to the particular problems associated with local authority involvement in companies. The company model is the main vehicle for conducting business in the private sector. However, the framework provided by company law is not sensitive to the needs of the public sector and gives rise to a range of problems for local authorities participating in companies (chapter 3). Coupled with this are the problems associated with the draconian system of regulation imposed on local authority involvement in companies linked to the controls imposed on capital finance (chapter 5).

The third, broader reason relates to the involvement of the private sector in the delivery of services traditionally provided by the public sector which continues to be a priority for the government. As a consequence the boundaries between the public and private sector become increasingly blurred with more emphasis placed on structures such as companies to induce private sector involvement. It becomes particularly important, in this context, to fully appreciate the problems that are raised when working through companies for elected members, local governance and public accountability.

Thus the focus of this report on companies is not in order to promote this particular model, but rather to enable councils to develop a better understanding of the various complex issues involved in using companies. The report looks at the areas where the use of local authority companies is likely to increase in the future as well as those areas where they have been used in the past (chapter 2). It discusses in detail the advantages and disadvantages for local authorities in using the company model (chapter 3) and explores the steps that can be taken to mitigate some of the problems. It does this in terms of good practice that can be adopted by local authorities within the existing frameworks (chapter 4) and beyond this it looks at the changes that are required to the legal and financial regulatory frameworks themselves (chapter 7).

In addressing the issues related to local authorities and companies, this report covers a highly technical area which has been affected substantially, although indirectly, by the introduction of the Local Government Acts of 1999 and 2000. The report aims to provide easily accessible information to a wide non-legal and legal audience in this complex area. It will be of use to councillors, helping them make informed choices on adopting new ways of delivering services and discharging functions that are required under the programme of local government reform. It will also be of use to officers with legal as well as strategic responsibilities in these areas. It needs to be stressed, however, that the information contained in this report is not a substitute for local authorities seeking expert advice on the many detailed legal and financial issues when considering the establishment of, or participation in, a company.

2 LOCAL AUTHORITY INVOLVEMENT IN COMPANIES

Local authorities may establish companies to serve a variety of purposes. The role of such companies can range from that of an agent, performing functions on behalf of the local authority to that of a clearly separate entity valued for its independence from the parent authority. Thus companies may be set up: to perform a co-ordinating function between different parties, in order for example to market a city; to act on behalf of one or more local authorities, in order for example to carry out procurement for the library service; or to engage in trading and other commercial activities.

This chapter looks at some of the areas where the use of local authority companies is likely to increase in the future as well as those areas where they have been used in the past. This does not mean, however, that companies are necessarily the best vehicles for undertaking partnership activities in these areas. In each case the local authority will have a wide range of choice on the structural options available (see chapter 6, page 57 for a discussion of different partnership structures). The aim of this chapter is to provide an indication of some of the different areas where the establishment of a local authority company may be worth considering.

Companies for trading

Where a local authority wishes to carry out discretionary activities for the benefit of its community, but needs to recover the costs incurred through charging or wishes to get a return on its investment in order to re-invest it for public benefit, the establishment of a company has certain advantages - for example, a company established to operate a car park. Such a company may be established by the local authority on its own or in partnership with other organisations.

This is likely to attract increasing interest in the light of the new power of well-being in the Local Government Act 2000 that allows local authorities greater freedom to explore innovative and creative ways of promoting the economic, social and environmental well-being of the community (see chapter 5, page 44 for discussion of the new power of wellbeing).

The well-being power encourages local authorities to work in partnership with other organisations but does not entitle these partnerships to charge for services. There are also restrictions imposed on the powers of local authorities to trade by the Local Authorities (Goods and Services) Act 1970. But a company as a separate entity is not subject to these restrictions. Where a local authority sets up a company under the well-being power, DETR guidance says that it can, unlike a local authority, charge for any services it provides to others (DETR (a), December 2000, paragraph 64).

Where a local authority establishes a company, on its own or in partnership with other organisations, in order to participate in any trading, development or other activities which might involve an element of speculation and risk, careful consideration will need to be given to issues such as accountability, propriety, conflicts of interest and personal liability (see page 21 for a discussion of these issues).

Companies for joint purchasing or supply

Some local authorities have combined resources on a region wide basis to establish joint arrangements for the purchase or supply of goods and services. Here, unlike the situation above, the main objective in establishing a company is to co-ordinate activities and to increase the efficiency with which statutory functions are discharged.

The advantage of this approach is that local authorities will be able to use their joint presence in the market to obtain discounts on purchases and re-invest surpluses from trading for the public benefit. This type of arrangement helps secure efficiency and economy and is likely to grow in importance under best value. Local authorities' powers to trade with other local authorities and specified public bodies as well as their ability to receive payment for those goods and services are specified under the Local Authorities (Goods and Services) Act 1970. The government intends to consult on proposals to extend these trading powers for best value purposes, using section 16 of the Local Government Act 1999 (see chapter 5, page 44 for further details).

Client side special purpose vehicle

Another situation where it may be appropriate for various organisations from the public sector within an area to join together is in order to funnel demand for a particular service. But the challenge is to find a way of bringing together various public bodies and potentially other organisations from the community and voluntary sectors to act in a concerted way as a purchaser of services.

The establishment of a company, in the form of a local authority led, client side, special purpose vehicle (SPV), could assist this task. Demand for a service could be channelled through the company so that the client side (or purchasing agent) can come to an agreement and speak with a single voice about what it is seeking to achieve, what the output specification should say and what benefits there should be for individual organisations that are participating in the company.

The Bates review of the PFI recommended this type of increased 'bundling' of projects to increase scale and thereby encourage greater participation of the private sector in PFI for local government.

Local Housing Companies

In the 90s a 'Local Housing Company' model was promoted by the Association of London Authorities, the Association of Metropolitan Authorities, the Association of District Councils and the LGIU. Under this model the stock was leased or transferred to a local authority controlled company. Tenants would remain secure tenants of the local authority. The company would finance investment by raising finance on the capital markets, underpinned by income from the rental stream. This model could only be successful if central government decided to amend the public expenditure rules and adopt the system of national accounts and classify these companies as 'corporations'.

Instead the Conservative Government introduced a new concept - the registered social landlord (RSL). This description encompassed housing associations and housing co-operatives. It also covered the Conservative government's version of a local housing company. These had to be companies limited by guarantee and registered under the Companies Act 1985. They also had to meet the registration requirements set by the Housing Corporation for RSLs.

However the Secretary of State exempted 'local housing companies' from being 'influenced' companies under Part V of the Local Government and Housing Act 1989, in order to enable one-third of the board to be members of the local authority (see page 51).

The aim was to provide a different form of vehicle that councils could sell (transfer) their housing to, as part of the programme of large scale voluntary transfer (LSVT) being promoted by the Government. A few local authorities have adopted this model, but most have followed the traditional route of creating a new housing association.

Arm's Length Housing Companies

The Housing Green Paper proposed the introduction of local authority controlled arm's length housing management companies (DETR(b), December 2000). Ownership of the housing stock would remain with the local authority and the local authority would remain the landlord. The government envisages that the arrangements will involve companies that will be 100 per cent controlled by the local authority, though it does not rule out options such as Industrial and Provident Societies. The government is not prescriptive about what functions should and should not be delegated but the consultation paper identifies those that are appropriate for delegation. They include:

● rent collection, arrears management and debt counselling

- tenant information, consultation and participation
- tenancy services and enforcement of tenancy conditions
- void and letting management
- stock investment decisions and repairs ordering
- estate management, caretaking and support services under supporting people.

Key features of these proposed companies include:

- Tenants remain as secure tenants of the local authority and their current rights are protected.
- The arrangements established in the locally agreed Tenants Compact will continue.
- Governance will be through a board consisting of councillors, tenants representatives and independent members. Councillors would not be in a majority. Board members may receive expenses but not fees.
- The local authority could be the sole shareholder or all the board members with the power to change the constitution of the company could be representatives of the local authority.
- Normally no more than 12,000 properties would be managed by a single body and where a local authority wished to apply these arrangements to more than 12,000 properties, a group structure would be appropriate with a parent body and area boards.
- Appropriate safeguards for employees' terms and conditions, including their pension rights.

Housing Regeneration Companies

The report of the Urban Task Force (Towards an urban renaissance, DETR, 1999) recommended the creation of joint enabling bodies in the form of Housing Regeneration Companies to facilitate a housing-led approach to regeneration. The idea behind the proposal is to facilitate Registered Social Landlords (RSLs) to work more freely in partnership with local authorities, private developers, local community groups and others. The remit of these joint venture organisations would be to regenerate through a combination of:

- acquisition of private sector housing for renovation and use either as tenanted social housing or for sale on shared

financial institutions   10.2%
eg banks (retail and investment) and insurance companies

other local authorities   28.2%

other public sector organisations   37.3%
eg colleges of further education, universities, the health service, the
voluntary sector and TECs.

Other local authorities and public sector organisations were found
to predominate. The latter group primarily consisted of TECs and
institutions of further education.

Reasons given by councils for establishing a company

When councils were asked to identify the reasons for creating a
company, the following picture emerged, ranked in order from the
most common to least common response:

- increase economic activity
- to obtain private sector involvement
- to obtain private sector funding
- commercial opportunity
- access to private sector market
- required by legislation
- to obtain private sector management
- seek value for money.

For details of the case studies used in the DETR research report see
the Appendix.

Benefits to local authorities of using companies

All incorporated bodies, whether they are companies established for not-for-profit purposes in the form of Industrial and Provident Societies or companies limited by guarantee, or companies limited by shares established for trading and other commercial purposes, share the following advantages:

- **Potential to bring together a wide range of interests in pursuit of common goals**

  Broadening the base of involvement in any area of activity can help to develop a better understanding of the relevant problems, leading to the development of more effective solutions. Involving different sectors in decision making helps to forge commitment across sectors.

- **Leverage and access to funds beyond the capability of the individual partner**

  Several funding regimes, such as the Single Regeneration Budget and various European Union programmes, require applicants to demonstrate a framework for partnership action. A company set up for bidding purposes need not necessarily carry out the programme itself if the bid for funding is successful.

- **Providing match funding**

  Certain types of public funding, such as lottery funding, government funding for regeneration and certain forms of funding forms of European funding, require match funding. Such match funding can be provided by a company which has local authority involvement.

- **Clear focus for achieving specific objectives**

  The creation of companies to pursue specific initiatives provides a focus for directors and management and, in turn, can facilitate the measurement of performance against identified objectives.

● **Increasing flexibility to achieve solutions**
Companies may offer the flexibility to local authorities to become more enterprising and business-like, characteristics which were said to be lacking in the formal local authority committee structure. However, it must be noted, changes being introduced to the political decision making structures in local authorities under Part 11 of the Local Government Act 2000 are likely to bring about radical change.

● **Access to wider skills base**
Establishing a partnership vehicle like a company provides an opportunity for councils to tap skills in both the commercial and not-for-profit sectors.

● **Separate legal identity**
Incorporation provides a company with its own, separate legal identity. This entitles the company to do such things as hold assets in its own name and take legal action in its own name.

● **Independence from each constituent partner**
Having a distinct identity separate from the constituent partners can be a distinct advantage in order, for example, to mobilise support for a new venture.

● **Limited liability**
A major factor in setting up a company is the desire to minimise any risk to the organisations and individuals involved in the venture. This is particularly important where the activity to be undertaken by the company involves financial risk. This includes companies established for trading, development and other commercial purposes.

In the event of the company becoming insolvent, the financial liability of the investors is limited to the value of their shareholding, for companies limited by shares, or to the amount they have agreed to guarantee, in the case of a company limited by guarantee.

● **Gaining the confidence of the business community**
Companies provide a framework that is well established and familiar for the private sector. Where it is important to get the support of the private sector for a particular venture this can be an advantage. Confidentiality and quick decision making are features of the company model that are favoured by the private sector.

Advantages of local authority led companies
All the above advantages apply together with the additional benefit of local authorities being able to exert a strong influence on the company. However, this means that the company will be subject to the stringent controls imposed by the local authority capital finance regime as well as the various rules on propriety (see chapter 5, page 55 and 56 for further details on these rules).

Advantages of private sector led companies

● **Free from controls on capital finance**
As a consequence of the statutory regulations imposed by the Local Government and Housing Act 1989 Act and the Local Authorities (Companies) Order 1995 there are incentives for authorities to be involved in non-regulated, rather than regulated, companies. By definition, non-regulated companies must be 'private sector led'. The main advantage to an authority of such joint ventures is that they are not caught by the capital finance provisions of the 1989 Act (see page 55 for details)

● **Access to private sector capital and funding**
A company that is not regulated can raise finance from banks or other lending institutions in the private sector unfettered by financial controls imposed over local authorities. The main reason for establishing a private sector led company is the

access that such a company has to private sector capital and funding. They are particularly relevant for large scale capital investment projects.

- **Opportunity to exploit a commercial opportunity**
  For example when Eurohub (Birmingham) was initially set up, the approach from British Airways was an essential part of the decision to pursue a joint venture (see appendix for details).

- **Access to wider public and private sector markets**
  For example Godiva Windows Ltd was set up by Coventry City Council when the successful Direct Labour Organisation (DLO) wanted to access wider public and private sector markets (see appendix for details).

- **Local authorities can participate in financial returns as a shareholder**
  Where the venture makes profit, as would be the objective of a private sector led company, the local authority would expect to get a return on it investment which could be used for public benefit.

Problems for local authorities in using companies

The company model is the main vehicle for conducting business in the private sector. Company law provides a well established and extensive framework for regulating all aspects of starting and running a company. This framework, however, is not sensitive to the needs of the public sector and gives rise to a range of problems for local authorities participating in companies. It is important for local authorities considering the use of companies to address these problems at the outset.

The problems are discussed below. In the next chapter (chapter 4) the steps that can be taken to mitigate some of these problems are explored.

Councillors and officers who are directors and conflict of interests
A councillor acting in the capacity of councillor, as well as an officer acting in the capacity of public servant, each has a fiduciary duty to act in the best interests of the council and its tax payers. When acting as directors of a company their primary responsibility is to the company not to council taxpayers. This is because directors of a company have a fiduciary duty to the company under company law which includes:

- the over riding duty to act in good faith in what they believe to be the interests of the company
- the duty to exercise their discretion independently
- the duty to avoid placing themselves in a position in which their personal interests or duties are liable to conflict with their duties to the company.

At times these two sets of duties, to the company and the council, may come into conflict. Under current company law the interest of the company must prevail even though for elected members and public servants, their responsibility to the council and ultimately to the public is likely to be paramount.

The following are some examples of situations that can give rise to conflicts of interest:

- Should a councillor who is a company director disclose to fellow councillors information about the company that is detrimental to the local community which may have been communicated to the individual in his/her capacity as director?

  Here the issue is about conflicting duties owed by the director to the company and the council. This issue also relates to the difficult challenge of balancing the need to protect confidentiality against the need to establish accountability.

  Article 7 of the Local Authorities (Companies) Order 1995 attempts to address this type of conflict issue for regulated companies. This provision requires information to be provided to council members about the company's affairs if a member reasonably requires it for the proper performance of duties. Disclosure is not required to be made if it would amount to a breach of statutory duty or would lead to a breach of confidence. Similar provision is made in respect of minority interest companies. However, difficult judgements would still need to be made in relation to protecting confidentiality and promoting the public interest.

- What happens when a council appointee who is a company director is mandated by a council committee to vote in a particular way on a matter to be decided by the board of directors of the company?

  Under company law directors are under a duty to exercise their discretion independently. A mandate of this kind, or a prior agreement, is a potential fetter on the directorís discretion and hence a possible breach of fiduciary duty owed to the company.

- What are the disclosure of interest obligations for council appointees who are company directors?

  There are higher standards of probity for local authorities than the private sector. Company law sets out the rules governing disclosure of personal interest by directors. But councillors are also governed by additional rules. These rules are currently contained in the National Code of Local Government Conduct 1990. This will soon be replaced by a new Code of Conduct as required under part 111 of the Local Government Act 2000, section 50. The initial commencement for the new Code of Conduct is expected to be July 2001. The Code will set out the rules on the declaration of pecuniary and non-pecuniary interests by individual councillors. A new Code of Conduct for local government employees will also be published as required by section 82 of the 2000 Act. The initial commencement for this too is expected to be July 2001. Currently, for local authority officers, the rules of s117 of the Local Government Act 1972 apply. These require any local authority officer who has a pecuniary interest, to declare it to the authority.

In the past establishing precisely if and when obligations arise which require the disclosure of certain interests was a tricky matter. To what extent the new Code will improve the situation remains to be seen. Where there are interests that need to be disclosed the individual should not take part in the decision-making process, or do so only in a limited manner

A large number of councillors serve as representatives of their local authorities on a wide range of outside bodies, including other public bodies, companies, charities and voluntary organisations. This has the potential for conflicts of interest to arise by virtue of their multiple roles. But if these councillors who are appointed to outside bodies are unduly prohibited from taking part in discussions concerning those bodies within their local authority they become excluded from making an informed contribution to the debate even though they may be best placed to do so.

In a limited number of areas, such as for directors of: transport and airport companies; City Challenge initiatives; and local authority waste disposal companies, some degree of government guidance has been provided on conflict issues. Companies set up for other purposes will need to establish their own rules.

The situation of potential conflict in duties is further complicated by the fact that there are different laws for different sectors (private, public and voluntary) making it difficult to establish precisely which duties and obligations are applicable at any given time. Different rules will apply depending on whether the individual is acting in the course of local authority, company or charity work. Other factors that have a bearing on the issue include the degree of local authority influence or control over the company and the precise purposes for which the company was formed and the purposes for which the individual director was appointed to act.

Personal liability of councillors and officers who are directors
Directors who are in breach of any duty imposed upon them by company law may personally be liable to reimburse to the company any profits made and/or losses suffered as a result. When insolvency threatens, liabilities towards creditors may arise for wrongful trading under insolvency legislation.

The obligations imposed by company law are onerous and there are severe penalties for non-compliance with many of the duties. It is therefore important for councillors and local authority officers appointed to act as company directors to ensure that they understand the duties and obligations the law imposes on them.

For example, a director is required to exercise reasonable skill and care in the performance of his or her duties commensurate with his or her knowledge and experience. All directors, including part-time or non-executive directors, are required to make themselves fully aware of the company's financial position and should attend Board meetings regularly. Ignorance of transactions entered into by the company through a failure to make proper enquiries may not be an adequate defence to a charge of negligence brought against such a director. Similarly, failure to attend Board meetings could lead to such a charge being brought.

Delegation of decision making
While a local authority can arrange for the delivery of a function through a company, it cannot delegate ultimate responsibility for that function. The delegation of decision making in local authorities is strictly controlled by law. Section 101 of the Local Government Act 1972 authorises a local authority to arrange for the discharge of any of its functions by a committee, sub-committee or an officer of the authority or by another local authority. These provisions have been supplemented by sections 14 to 20 of the Local Government Act 2000 which set out the delegation of executive functions under

the new decision making structures introduced in the 2000 Act. The 2000 Act authorises a local authority to arrange for the discharge of its executive functions by the whole executive, a member of the executive, a committee of the executive or an officer of the authority or, subject to regulation by the secretary of state, by an area committee of that authority. An authority cannot arrange for the discharge of its functions by any other person, which would include a company or an individual director.

The Deregulation and Contracting Out Act 1994 provides an avenue, under certain circumstances, for a local authority wishing to delegate a function. It allows the local authority to authorise any person to exercise a function and whatever is then carried out by that person is treated as if it had been carried out by the authority itself. But this avenue is only available for functions that are not 'excluded' in the 1994 Act. In addition it requires the Secretary of State to provide for such delegation by order. Only a limited number of orders have so far been made.

Council provided support services
When a company is established it may require support services from the local authority, such as accounting and legal advice and administrative back up. For companies that are established under the well-being power, provisions in the Local Government Act 2000 enable local authorities to make available such services. The DETR draft guidance on the well-being power (DETR(a), December 2000) states that financial assistance under the well-being power can take any form including the provision of staff, goods and services and accommodation ie contributions can be made 'in kind' (see page 44 for further details). However, the limit on raising money contained in section 3(2) of the Local Government Act 2000 means that local authorities can not rely on the well-being power to charge for any such contribution that they make.

For companies that are established for other purposes there may be constraints on the provision of goods and services by local authorities. The Local Authorities (Goods and Services) Act 1970 enables authorities to only provide certain categories of services to organisations having 'public body status'. If the company has public body status then the types of service that may be provided by the authority to the company include the supply of goods and materials, the provision of administrative, professional and technical services, and maintenance work. But a local authority company does not automatically have 'public body status' as defined by section 1(4) of the 1970 Act. In the absence of such status an authority's powers to provide services to the company may be constrained.

The list of public bodies with whom local authorities are allowed to trade is being reviewed and consolidated currently as part of the best value regime and this should greatly help with removing uncertainty in this area.

Establishing democratic accountability
The very independence and separate status of a company that makes it an attractive option also brings with it the danger of eroding democratic accountability. The need to observe confidentiality and protect commercial interests has to be carefully weighed against the need to establish democratic accountability and protect public interests.

Managing a mix of commercial and community objectives
For local authorities improving the quality of life of their community is of paramount importance. This requires local authorities to take a strategic and holistic approach to all the activities they engage in, assessing impact in a multidimensional manner. Thus local authorities will be concerned about the impact of their activities on the economic, social, cultural and environmental well-being of their community, in its widest sense.

The decision to adopt a company structure to undertake an activity will usually be related to meeting commercial objectives, often in partnership with the private sector. In such situations managing this mix of commercial and community objectives can prove to be a problem. There is inherent tension between the need of the private sector to get maximum return on its investment in the form of financial rewards for shareholders, and the need for the public sector to get maximum impact in terms of economic, social, cultural and environmental benefit for the community.

Workforce issues
Where companies are established local government workers may regard them with suspicion. This is wholly understandable in that Compulsory Competitive Tendering is remembered most for the effect it had, not on improvements in the quality of services, but on public sector jobs and national terms and conditions of employment, especially those of women and part-time workers.

Despite central government's attempts to soften the blow and to take account of the concerns of public sector workers, the same dangers are emerging with new partnership arrangements under best value and PFI leading to the creation of a two-tier workforce. Where staff have been transferred from the local authority to a different entity, the Transfer of Undertakings (Protection of Employment) Regulations (TUPE) protects their terms and conditions of employment. But new employees are invariably paid less than the transferred staff. They have worse conditions and are likely to work longer hours for less pay. They rarely have access to pensions and, when they do, it is certainly not a 'broadly comparable' scheme that is on offer.

Transferred staff, who are ostensibly protected, also see pay and conditions reduced over time, with 'economic, technical or organisational' (ETO) reasons being used to justify them. Only on a small number of IT-related contracts, where men tend to be a larger proportion of the workforce and where the labour market is tight, do national terms and conditions seem to be maintained.

This bodes ill for women workers, but just as badly for the quality of services provided. Efficiency savings may be easy to achieve through cuts to the pay and pensions bill, but quality is just as likely to be squeezed out under commercial pressures.

Casualisation of the labour force is also commonplace with an increasing tendency to employ staff on a temporary basis, as and when required rather than on secure, permanent contracts.

The next chapter explores the steps that can be taken to mitigate some of the problems described above.

4 CHECK LIST FOR SETTING UP AND USING COMPANIES

The problems associated with local authorities working through companies were discussed in the previous chapter. This chapter looks at the steps that can be taken to mitigate some of those problems and other issues that need to be considered when establishing and using companies.

Before arriving at a decision on setting up a company the following questions should be answered:

Which structure will best suit need?

There are a wide variety of organisational structures that a local authority can choose from when setting up a partnership or embarking on a new activity. These include an informal partnership, a trust, an industrial and provident society, a controlled or influenced company or a company that is neither controlled or influenced (see chapter 6 on page 57 for information on different partnership structures). The choice of structure will depend largely on:

1. what the local authority wants to achieve. For example, is the new structure being created:
   - to promote a city?
   - to raise issues of concern within a community?
   - to bid for funds from grant distributing agencies?
   - to provide a vehicle through which different parties can work together?
   - to attract funds from the private sector?
   - to reduce costs in the delivery of services, through for example, better procurement arrangements?
   - to utilise collective purchasing power?
   - to improve efficiency in the delivery of services, through for example, pooling resources and expertise from different organisations?
   - to create an entity that enables the community to benefit from a development?

- to make profit through trading or through the exploitation of other commercial opportunities?

2.   how the local authority intends to use the new structure to achieve these objectives. For example:
- has it been created for 'not-for-profit' purposes?
- is it expected to hold assets or enter into contracts?
- how important is it, for the partners concerned, that the organisation created has a separate and independent identity of its own?
- how important is it, in relation to general public perception, that the organisation created has a separate and independent identity of its own?
- will it be financially free standing, in that it will be financed and supported entirely from the resources which each party to the venture contributes, plus any income derived from other sources such as trading activities or grant funding?
- will it require additional finance from central government sources?

Does the council have the necessary statutory power?
Until the passing of the Local Government Acts of 1999 and 2000, one of the biggest technical challenges faced by councils wishing to create and participate in partnerships was the identification of appropriate powers (see page 41 for discussion of vires). The lack of legal certainty was a particular problem for private sector institutions investing in these partnership projects.

The recent changes introduced through the best value regime (see page 44) and the new power of well-being (see page 44) facilitate partnership working by local authorities. It is still necessary, however, to carefully appraise each project in order to ensure that it is covered by the provisions of current legislation and complies with their requirements.

What will be the tax implications of setting up a company?
The tax liabilities, in relation to for example VAT, Corporation Tax and Capital Gains Tax, can be very different for local authorities,

trusts, not for profit companies and companies that trade to make a surplus. Therefore it is important to carry out a detailed analysis of the tax implications before making the decision to establish a new company.

Is there a business plan?

A well thought out business plan is an essential first step in creating a new partnership. A good business plan will include information on: cash flow forecasts; tax considerations; estimates of the cash generation potential (if any); the peaks and troughs of working capital; the impact of future capital expenditure; the availability (or otherwise) of grant funding; the services the business intends to offer; the marketing arrangements; the operational performances the business intends to meet; the management proposals for financing arrangements and future prospects. It should also set out the key objectives which the business must achieve and will need to contain sufficient information to enable a third party (such as a bank) to make a decision as to whether to advance money to the new venture and (if this is a factor) whether this can be achieved by secured or unsecured lending. Most importantly, the business plan should look at all eventualities and consider 'down side risk' as well as more optimistic forecasts of the undertaking's commercial potential (based on information from Butterworths).

Once it is decided that the establishment of a company is the best option and the council has the legal capacity to establish and participate in such a company, a series of further questions need to be addressed. These reflect the problems that were discussed in detail in the previous chapter (see pages 21-29).

How are conflict of interest issues to be resolved?

Procedures need to be developed to deal with conflict of interest problems (see page 22 for a discussion of these problems). One way of doing this is to set out in the Articles of Association of the company a protocol for the declaration of interests by directors and procedures on how to handle potential situations of conflict of interest. The procedures should cover areas such as: the disclosure of information by council appointed directors to the company and to other elected members of the council; and the decision making role of council appointed directors when transactions involving the council are being considered by the company. It may be relevant to adopt the new Code of Conduct on these issues that local authorities will be required to sign up to under the provisions contained in Part III of the Local Government Act 2000.

In a joint venture company a shareholders agreement that sets out the duties and responsibilities of each party may be used to clarify procedures on these issues.

What steps have been taken to protect council appointed directors from personal liability?

Since officers and councillors who are also company directors may be exposed to personal liability under certain situations it is important to ensure that insurance cover is in place to provide compensation for any loss that may arise.

It may be possible for the council itself to protect such individuals through indemnities or insurance policies provided the following two conditions are met:

- there are clear statutory enabling powers for the authority to be involved with the company and
- the council appointees are acting in the course of their local government employment or carrying out public duties on behalf of the council.

However, in the case of councillors acting for external agencies, even where they are carrying out public duties, there is some uncertainty as to whether there are powers for local authorities to provide indemnities. To clear this uncertainty the government has promised, following consultation, to make an order under section 101 of the Local Government Act 2000 conferring power on local authorities to provide such indemnities (DETR(a), December 2000, paragraph 34).

Most insurance policies of this kind for officers and directors that are available in the market are renewable annually and will exclude certain risks. Where they are used they will need to be regularly updated. The activities carried out by the directors should be monitored to ensure that they are covered by the terms of the policy.

How will councillors who are directors be supported?

Where the council has appointed elected members as directors, structures should be put in place to support them in this role. One way of doing this is to identify a lead officer within the local authority to support each councillor who has been appointed as a company director. Such a support officer may be appointed as an alternative director to an elected member director. This ensures that the officer receives papers, is able to attend meetings when necessary and is kept fully up to date.

This support role is an important one. But it needs to be handled carefully because executive directors have a duty to exercise their discretion independently and company law contains provisions to identify and penalise 'shadow directors' who usurp the role of executive directors.

What level of ethical standards and financial probity will be appropriate?

Public bodies are required to abide by higher levels of ethical standards and financial probity than private organisations. The ethical framework introduced under Part III of the Local Government Act 2000 requires local authorities to adopt a code of conduct and establish standards committees. Two new independent bodies funded by central government, the Standards Board for England and one for Wales, will also be established which will employ Ethical Standards Officers to investigate allegations of a breach of the Code of Conduct by councillors. Although a company, which is a separate entity from a local authority, is not required to abide by the same rules on ethical standards as a local authority, it would be good practice to do so as far as is practical.

Where the company is not controlled or influenced are there other mechanisms to protect the public interest?

In those cases where a company is neither controlled nor influenced there may be other mechanisms through which the public interest can be protected. These include the terms of leases where the company is operating from buildings owned by the local authority and grant conditions where the company receives payments from the local authority.

How will public accountability be established?

Balancing the establishment of public accountability with the need to protect confidentiality can be tricky. Local authority companies would be expected to adopt openness as a principle, within the bounds of commercial confidentiality, in their dealings with all interested parties.

The Cadbury Code of Best Practice published in December 1992 lays down certain requirements with regard to company annual reports and accounts which should be seen as a minimum. Such reports should be made available to all elected members.

The Cadbury Code requires companies to report on systems of internal control. Local authorities use set financial regulations as one mechanism for internal control. This is not a practice that is common amongst smaller private sector companies. It is useful to ensure that local authority companies operate within a codified framework of financial control. This can be based on existing local authority financial regulations tailored to meet the needs of the particular company. These regulations include provisions for:

- effective means of securing competition in the procurement of goods and services, as defined by European Union procurement procedures,
- a risk-averse approach towards cash-flow management and investment backed by a risk management strategy.

Guidance on financial practice for local authorities with interests in companies is available from The Accounting Standards Board and CIPFA.

It is important for local authority companies to have effective systems for audit and review and an appropriate corporate governance framework. The DETR good practice guide (DETR(b), November 1997) recommends that an independent external auditor should be appointed with right of access to the company's records so that they can follow the trail of public money. In addition, the report suggests there should be an internal audit function even though this is something that most small and medium sized companies in the private sector would not have. The internal audit function may be contracted on a part-time basis from the local authority. The company should have an audit committee, even if it is the full Board meeting as a committee, to receive reports from the external and internal auditors.

How will councillors monitor the performance of the company?

Appropriate reporting arrangements need to be put in place to ensure that elected members of the local authority are kept informed about the company's activities and progress. Where the authority is a customer of the company as well as a stakeholder partner, it is essential to have two separate reporting arrangements to reflect these two different roles.

Shareholder reports, prepared by the company for its various partners, should be available to all councillors to provide them with the opportunity to be kept informed. However such reports need to respect commercial confidence.

Councils have adopted different approaches to reporting in the past. The DETR study (DETR(a) 1997) described the following examples: Coventry City Council had a shareholder panel made up of councillors who met on a regular basis to receive reports from company directors that the council had appointed. Kirklees MBC had a scrutiny commission to review its partnership activity.

The new political management structures being put in place in local authorities under Part 11 of the Local Government Act 2000 require the separation of the executive and scrutiny roles of the council. The draft guidance on the well-being power (DETR(a), December 2000, Annex on executive arrangements) states that 'the executive - as the clear, accountable, corporate leadership for the council - will lead the search for best value and be the focus for partnership working with other local public, private and voluntary sector bodies'. Arrangements need to be put in place to ensure effective scrutiny of this function by non-executive members.

Even where the main objective of the company is commercial, local authorities would want to monitor the wider economic, social and environmental impact of the activities of the company on the community. This should be done in relation to the community plan which local authorities are required to produce under the Local Government Act 2000 as part of promoting the well-being of their area.

How will staff be protected?
Where the company intends to employ staff and the company is engaged in functions that were previously undertaken by the local authority or another public body it is likely that the company will inherit existing staff. It will be of paramount importance that any staff the company inherits, through a TUPE transfer or other means, are as positive about their own future prospects as are the architects of the new company. Discussion at the earliest possible stage with any staff affected, together with their trade union representatives, will ensure that issues such as jobs, pay and conditions, training, union recognition and pension rights will be as openly and thoroughly considered as is necessary to forestall rumours and speculation which may be damaging to staff morale and the future success of the company.

On which issues will expert advice be needed?
Apart from the above issues that councils will need to scrutinise particularly carefully, there are several technical issues related to the formation of a company on which expert legal and financial advice would be required. These include (based on information from):

- ensuring that the council has the legal capacity to establish and participate in the company

- drafting of the Memorandum and Articles of Association and deciding on whether additional joint venture or shareholder agreements are necessary
- deciding on how and on what basis partners may leave the company
- agreeing the number and make-up of the board of directors and the extent of its delegated authority taking account of Part V of the 1989 Act and the 1995 Order
- agreeing the extent to which the company's activities are to be insured and insurance arrangements put in place for directors
- terms of leases and grant conditions
- reviewing the tax environment within which the partnership will operate and ensuring the avoidance of unnecessary tax burden
- devising an appropriate funding structure, like for example the correct level of debt equity mix for a large scale joint venture
- arrangements for delivering community benefits
- assessing funding proposals from prospective partners for their feasibility.

What council resources will be needed to set up a company?

There are various local authority resource issues that need to be addressed right at the beginning of the process of setting up a company. These are fully discussed in the DETR good practice guide (DETR(b), November 1997).

Seeing an initiative through from vision to implementation requires commitment and significant staff resources. Achieving success is aided by the commitment of cross-departmental resources, including legal and financial expertise. Equally, expertise in the relevant service or function and good project management skills are necessary.

Funding for these resources, and specialist input as appropriate, will be necessary for the council to develop the initiative to a position where they can approach the other potential partners.

5 CURRENT DEVELOPMENTS AND THE LEGAL FRAMEWORK

Background to the development of legal restrictions on the involvement of local authorities in companies

During the 1980s local authorities were facing new restrictions - particularly financial controls that affected capital investment - and were losing functions to quangos. Forward looking local authorities sought to establish innovative ways to bringing benefit to their communities through extending their areas of activities. One of the avenues used was the establishment and use of companies. Establishing a company that could for example, acquire an asset and lease it to a local authority or could have an asset owned by the local authority leased to it, enabled local authorities to develop new opportunities.

One attraction of this option lay in the independent status of companies once they are incorporated. Under company law, persons who form and control companies have freedom to set the rules for the company as they see fit. A company in which a local authority had an interest appeared to be free, within the wide limits available under company law, to diverge from the rules applying to local authorities.

During this period central government pursued a strategy to reduce public expenditure through repeated attempts to control expenditure by local authorities and remove functions from organisations that were democratically accountable and transfer them to quangos.

The ability of local authorities to use companies to, for example, borrow money on the financial markets was perceived as a threat to central control. Such borrowing, although generally underwritten by local authorities by way of guarantees and/or indemnities, would not count as local authority 'borrowing' and therefore did not score against the local authorities' respective prescribed expenditure totals.

The Committee of Inquiry into the Conduct of Local Authority Business set up under the chairmanship of David Widdicombe in 1986 raised further concerns about the powers of local authorities to have interests in companies, the lack of transparency and accountability to the parent authority and the fact that such bodies were not subject to the same disciplines on finance and propriety as apply to ordinary mainstream local authority activities.

Against this background two parallel sets of developments occurred that were to severely curtail the ability of local authorities to enter into partnership arrangements in general, and company structures in particular. These were: the enactment by the government of Part V of the Local Government and Housing Act 1989; and the adoption by the courts of a very narrow construction on the issue of local authority powers that led to uncertainty over the legal capacity of local authorities to establish or participate in companies.

Controls imposed through the capital finance system
In order to control local authorities and their involvement in companies the government enacted Part V of the Local Government & Housing Act 1989 (see page 51). The legislation defined a company where a local authority had more than 50 per cent of the board or shares as a controlled company and a company where a local authority had 20 per cent or more of the seats on the board or the shares as an influenced company. Critically the legislation counted any capital expenditure by controlled or influenced companies as expenditure by the authority. At a time when capital expenditure was being severely restricted councils now faced a situation where capital expenditure by companies would mean that capital expenditure on other projects could not take place.

Although the provisions of the 1989 Act did not come into force until the 1995 Local Authorities (Companies) Order was made, the Act had an inhibitory impact on local authorities from the time it was passed.

The controls that were introduced on the capital finance system succeeded in curtailing the ability of local authorities to raise funds for capital expenditure, which was the government's primary objective. But they also had the effect of preventing the creation of partnerships with the private sector which the government was keen to encourage. The system of control imposed was so draconian that it began to stifle local authority initiative and prevent the development of innovative and effective solutions to emerging problems.

The issue of ultra vires
The legal concept of ultra vires relates to circumstances in which a body such as a company or a local authority is said to be acting beyond the legitimate scope of its activities. The application of the doctrine of ultra vires protects local tax payers from any speculative and unlawful activity carried out by a local authority. However, it leaves third parties entering into transactions with local authorities in good faith unprotected. If a local authority enters into a transaction which is subsequently held to be ultra vires, the agreement will be null and void, meaning that neither party can sue under the 'contract'.

In the 1980s and 90s a number of high profile court actions against local authorities were brought by banks and other lending institutions seeking to enforce, for example, interest rate swap agreements, guarantees, loan agreements or indemnities which authorities had entered into. But they discovered to their cost that the powers under which the local authorities had been acting were open to question. A number of these cases had in common the fact that a company was established to perform the function in question. As a result of these cases a crisis of confidence developed, on the part of both the private sector and local authorities, over the use of companies for partnership schemes.

Prior to the raising of the profile of local authority companies and powers issues, it had generally been assumed that local authorities had the power to establish a company. They did so, on the basis of a combination of powers, usually s137 of the Local Government Act1972 (which enabled local authorities to spend a limited budget on activities which it considered to be for the benefit of its local inhabitants) and s111 of the 1972 Act (which enabled a local authority to do anything 'which is calculated to facilitate, or is conducive or incidental to, the discharge of any of their functions'). However this ceased to be the case since the courts construed s111 narrowly. Thus the issue of identifying a power before being able to establish a company for a particular function became a difficult, complex and often uncertain matter, involving the careful scrutiny of the precise wording of statutes, regulations and other enactments, concerning the activity in question. This had the effect of discouraging partnership activities.

Private Finance Initiative (PFI) and conflicting trends
In the early 1990s, however, government policy began to change to actively encourage partnership arrangements as part of a wide range of urban policy initiatives to facilitate closer working, particularly between the public and private sectors. The substitution of borrowing by the private sector on the capital markets for public sector borrowing from the same capital markets to finance capital projects became, and remains, a major central government policy objective.

The Private Finance Initiative was launched in 1992. Central government's desire to reduce public expenditure did not just mean shifting the costs of local services to local taxpayers. Cutting capital expenditure (or financing capital investment differently) was an easy way to cut public expenditure, and the way the accounts worked simply made it more attractive if the objective was to cut 'headline' public spending. For example, if the government borrowed £5 million in order to build a new hospital, the public accounts would not only include the £5 million spent in the year it was built, but would also include, in future years, the debt charges and interest on the loans as they were repaid.

PFI was a new way of buying services that were capital intensive. Instead of the government borrowing from the private sector, with central government departments financing construction projects and then operating the services, the private sector would be invited not only to finance the construction but also to provide some or all of the services associated with the project. In return the government would pay for the services over a period of years and these fees would include the costs associated with the capital investment.

This was attractive to the government as there was no need to make provision within the public expenditure figures for the capital costs. It was designed to enable the government to proceed with investment in major capital projects.

A whole raft of regulations in four separate tranches were introduced during 1995-1997 to mitigate the effect of the capital finance regime to facilitate certain types of transaction under PFI. A wholesale consolidation of all the changes was carried out and brought into force in 1997. Yet, the controls imposed on the capital finance system through Part V of the 1989 Act which were stifling partnership working, continued then (and continue now) to be in place.

There have also been legislative pressures on local authorities to create company structures in specific areas. Examples include the Transport Act 1985, under which councils wishing to continue with bus operations had to establish distinct subsidiaries, and the Environmental Protection Act 1990, with a similar requirement to establish Local Authority Waste Disposal Companies and the Airports Act 1986 with the requirement to establish public airport companies.

Current developments affecting partnership working by local authorities

The current Labour Government that came to power in 1997 has had partnership working as a key plank of its public policy. It has put in place new legislation that has the potential to significantly increase the degree of flexibility that local authorities have in relation to the way in which they can structure and plan for the fulfilment of their functions. This includes the option to establish or participate in new organisational structures such as charitable trusts or profit making companies when appropriate.

Best Value
The Local Government Act 1999 imposes a new duty of best value on local authorities to secure continuous improvement in the way in which their functions are exercised. It is designed to challenge traditional assumptions about how services can be delivered through exploring new and more efficient ways. In order to make this possible the government has recognised the need to make a wider variety of service delivery vehicles available so that local authorities are not restricted unnecessarily as to how they secure best value. Partnerships are encouraged to play a central and increasingly important role in this process.

Section 16 of the 1999 Act is the key provision that can potentially provide local authorities with the necessary powers to experiment with different structures and methods of delivering services to the public. Section 16 enables the government to modify existing enactments as well as confers on local authorities new powers which it considers necessary or expedient to achieve best value. However this power is constrained in an important way by residing with the Secretary of State rather than with local authorities. It is the Secretary of State who will decide which statutory obstructions to best value will be modified or excluded, as well as which new powers will be granted to facilitate best value.

Although the best value framework came into force in April 2000, many of the legislative details are being gradually developed through the use of secondary legislation. A consultation paper is expected shortly on proposed regulations to confer additional powers on best value authorities under section 16 of the 1999 Act. To what extent the potential of section 16 will be actually fulfilled remains to be seen.

The new power of well-being
Part 1 of the Local Government Act 2000 provides for a new power for local authorities to promote the economic, social and environmental wellbeing of the community. This wide-ranging power is designed to be a 'power of first resort'. The DETR draft guidance to the well-being power (DETR(a), December 2000, paragraph 11)

states 'rather than hunting for a specific power elsewhere in statute in order to take a particular action, councils can instead look to the well-being power in the first instance'. The creation of the new power confers a new function on local government, namely that of promoting or improving community well-being (paragraph 14).

The power of well-being came into force on 18 October 2000. It represents an important development in enabling new types of partnerships to be established. Complementing the provisions of the 1999 Act, the new power of well-being will encourage local authorities to explore new approaches to carrying out their functions and enable them to choose from a wider range of vehicles for doing so.

The new power is intended to be a wide-ranging one which will enable local authorities to take action to improve the quality of life and health of their local communities. Specific examples of the kind of action that can be taken are set out in section 2(4) of the Act. These include the power of local authorities to:
  a) incur expenditure
  b) give financial assistance to any person
  c) enter into arrangements or agreements with any person
  d) co-operate with, or facilitate or co-ordinate the activities of any person
  e) exercise on behalf of any person any functions of that person, and
  f) provide staff, goods, services or accommodation to any person.

However, this is not an exhaustive list and does not limit in any way how local authorities can use the new power.

There is no limitation on the amount of money a local authority can spend. Authorities will be able to fund the activities of different groups and bodies, as well as invest in such activities, if they consider that this expenditure contributes to the economic, social or environmental well-being of the local area. Such financial assistance may be given by any means that authorities consider appropriate, including by way of grants or loans, or by the provision of guarantees (DETR(a), December 2000, paragraph 33).

In addition to providing financial assistance, councils are also permitted to provide other forms of assistance, including staff, goods and services and accommodation under section 2(4)(f) of the 2000 Act. This, according to the draft guidance, means that local authorities can make such a contribution 'in kind' (DETR(a), December 2000, paragraph 40).

Limitations on the well-being power are set out in section 3(1) which states that 'the power under section 2(1) does not enable a local authority to do anything that they are unable to do by virtue of any prohibition, restriction or limitation on their powers which is contained in any enactment (whenever passed or made)'. This means that under the new power of well-being councils are able to undertake any activity that promotes the well-being of their area, except where they are specifically restricted from doing so by any prohibition, restriction or limitation spelt out in other legislation.

The regulation of local authority involvement in companies has not been altered by the new power of well-being. Where a council decides to use a company as a means of promoting well-being it will still need to fully comply with the controls imposed by Part V of the Local Government and Housing Act 1989, the Local Authority Companies Order 1995 and the Local Authority (Capital Finance) Regulation 1997 (see pages 51-56).

Where a council finds that it is prevented from exercising the well-being power by the requirements of other legislation, the 2000 Act provides a remedy. Section 5 of the 2000 Act enables the Secretary of State to amend, repeal or revoke restrictions that obstruct the use of the well-being power.

This power adds to the existing powers under section 16 of the 1999 Act (see above) which enables the Secretary of State to modify or exclude legislation that prevents local authorities from achieving best value and to confer new powers on best value authorities for this purpose. This gives the minister wide powers and it has been expected that it will be used to ease some of the current constraints on partnerships.

While the well-being power is confined to principal councils, the powers in section 16 can be used to confer new powers on all best value authorities, including police, fire and passenger transport authorities as well as principal councils.

Limits on raising money and charging for services
The well-being power does not enable a local authority to raise money, whether by precepts, borrowing or otherwise (section 3(2)). This broadly drafted restriction seeks to ensure that a local authority can only obtain funds to pursue well-being objectives through existing sources of income.

This restriction also prevents local authorities from using the well-being power to charge for services they provide in pursuit of well-being objectives. This is likely to discourage partnership working by councils since they will be unable to recover costs incurred in promoting well-being through innovative initiatives, unless greater flexibility to charge is introduced in other legislation.

The government recognises that there is a case for local authorities to have greater ability to charge for discretionary services than they currently enjoy. The government therefore proposes that regulations should be made under section 150 of the Local Government and Housing Act 1989 to provide local authorities with power to charge for certain discretionary services, including those provided by virtue of the well-being power. Work will begin on these regulations in 2001 following the consultation on local government finance (DETR(a), December 2000, paragraph 63).

The draft guidance provides the following clarification in relation to companies set up under the well-being power:

● Charging - where an authority chooses to use its power

under section 2 to set up a company, that company as a separate entity is not subject to the restrictions provided by section 3(2). In practice, this means that such a company can charge for any services it provides to others (DETR(a), December 2000, paragraph 64).

● Power to trade - Local authorities' powers to trade with other local authorities and specified public bodies as well as their ability to receive payment for those goods and services are specified under the Local Authorities (Goods and Services) Act 1970. These powers are not affected by the new power of well being in the 2000 Act. The government intends to consult on proposals to extend these trading powers for best value purposes, using section 16 of the Local Government Act 1999 (DETR(a), December 2000, paragraph 64)

Power to form companies and other corporate bodies
The draft guidance puts beyond doubt the power of councils to form companies and other corporate bodies (paragraphs 41- 44). It states that the well-being power will enable local authorities to form or invest in companies, trusts, or charities, including joint venture companies, provided that they are satisfied that formation of, or participation in, a particular company is likely to achieve the promotion or improvement of the economic, social or environmental well-being of the authority's area.

It also provides clarification on the receipt of dividends by local authorities. Where participation in a company gives rise to dividend payment to the authority as a shareholder, it is the government's view that such dividends would not amount to raising money for the purposes of section 3(2) (DETR(a), December 2000, paragraph 41).

However, formation of and participation in companies, as mentioned above, will be subject to the control mechanisms set out in Part V of the Local Government and Housing Act 1989 and the accompanying Local Authorities (Companies) Order 1995.

The well-being provisions not only confer new powers on councils to achieve a certain end (the promotion of well-being), they also expand the range of means available to councils to pursue that end. So, in pursuit of well-being, councils are able to establish companies and other forms of corporate body, to create pooled budgets, to undertake lead or joint commissioning, and to integrate the provision of their services with those of other service providers.

It is the government's intention to extend these provisions beyond a council's efforts to promote well-being to apply equally to any and all of its other functions. According to the draft guidance this will be done through guidance to section 16 of the 1999 Act that is expected to be published shortly.

Removal of legislative barriers to the promotion of well-being
Section 5 of the 2000 Act gives the Secretary of State the power to amend, repeal, revoke or disapply any enactment which he considers 'prevents or obstructs local authorities from exercising their power'. This power adds to the Secretary of State's existing power under section 16 of the Local Government Act 1999 to modify or exclude enactments that prevent authorities from achieving best value and to confer new powers on best value authorities for this purpose.

Economic development powers
The 2000 Act repeals the economic development powers contained in sections 33 to 35 of the Local Government and Housing Act 1989. Section 33 gave local authorities specific authority to set up and participate in companies for the purpose of economic development. With the introduction of the well-being power, section 33 (and the accompanying regulatory provisions in sections 34 and 35) are no longer needed. Sections 34 and 35 were repealed on 18 October 2000. Section 33 will be repealed on 28 July 2001 (DETR(a), December 2000, paragraph 44).

This repeal means that local authorities are no longer required to produce an annual report on the use of the economic development power. In future local authorities need to integrate the development of their economic development and regeneration work within the framework of the well-being power.

Section 137 of the Local Government Act 1972 has also been repealed since it has been superseded by the new power to promote well-being, except in the case of parish and community councils, which will not have the new power. Before the passing of the Local Government and Housing Act of 1989 economic development expenditure accounted for a substantial proportion of local authority expenditure under section 137. Since 1989 it has largely been used for community projects. The well-being power enables local authorities to incur expenditure. But, unlike section 137, the 2000 Act imposes no limit on the amount of money a local authority can spend in promoting well-being.

Indemnities
The draft guidance states that the government does not consider that the well-being power enables authorities to grant indemnities against personal financial loss to their members or officers in all the circumstances in which such indemnities would be appropriate (DETR(a), December 2000, paragraph 34). In order to put this issue beyond doubt, the government intends, following consultation, to make an order under section 101 of the 2000 Act conferring power on local authorities to provide such indemnities.

Encouraging change
The government has also introduced local Public Service Agreements (PSAs) to explore how any relaxation in the statutory or administrative framework and financial incentives can drive changes in service delivery. Local authorities who sign up to local PSAs will agree to meet challenging targets to deliver national or local priorities, in return for greater operational freedom and flexibility, some up-front financial incentives and rewards for success. At least some of the freedoms and flexibilities sought are likely to require use of the provisions in section 5 of the 2000 Act. There are currently 20 authorities piloting the scheme. Subject to evaluation of the pilot, the government intends to extend local PSAs, on a voluntary basis, to other top-tier authorities from 2001 and to district councils thereafter.

The government has also recently issued draft non-statutory guidance on the creation of 'local strategic partnerships' (LSPs) which are designed to be umbrella bodies within which other partnerships within a particular locality can be co-ordinated. If councils, and LSPs, think the well-being of their localities can be improved by amending or disapplying certain legislative requirements, section 5 of the 2000 Act will allow the Secretary of State to enable this (DETR, October 2000, paragraph 3.14). However, the draft guidance states 'Ministers will want reassurance that individual LSPs meet certain minimum criteria before considering requests for freedoms and flexibilities' (paragraph 3.1). It is not clear at this stage what these criteria will be.

The regulatory framework for local authority involvement in companies

Where a local authority participates in a company (limited by shares or guarantee) or an Industrial and Provident Society, the position is regulated by Part V of the Local Government and Housing Act 1989 and the Local Authorities (Companies) Order 1995.

The legislation divided the type of companies in which local authorities have an interest into regulated and non-regulated companies. Regulated companies are treated as being part of the local authority itself for capital finance purposes and are subject to the most stringent controls. Unregulated companies are not subject to the capital finance regime and their assets and the private finance raised by them do not score against public expenditure limits. This has meant that local authorities in establishing companies have had to spend much effort in ensuring that they do not fall into the regulated category.

Part V of the Local Government and Housing Act 1989 and the Local Authorities (Companies) Order 1995
The 1989 Act introduced different categories of local authority companies: controlled, influenced, arm's length or minority interest. The category the company falls under is determined by an analysis of the association between the authority and the company. The primary tests of association are:

- the distribution of voting rights
- the constitution of the board
- the powers of the authority to appoint or remove directors, and
- the business relationship existing between the authority and the company.

When the 1995 Order was introduced the additional test of 'effective control' became the key element in determining the status of a company. Under the 1995 Order the main distinction is not between controlled, influenced or minority interest companies but between private sector influenced companies that are 'effectively controlled' by the private sector - which are not regulated, and public sector influenced companies that are 'effectively controlled' by the public sector - which are regulated ie subject to local authority capital finance and propriety rules (see page 55).

Regulated companies
Public sector influenced companies that are 'effectively controlled' by a local authority are regulated (subject to local authority capital finance or propriety rules).
In broad terms, a local authority company is deemed to be regulated if:
- it is a controlled company or
- it is a local authority influenced company that satisfies either
  - the effective control test or
  - it would be required to prepare group accounts for the company in question.

Controlled companies
A controlled company is one in which one or more of the following applies:
- where the local authority holds more than 50 per cent of the voting rights in the company, or
- where the local authority has power to appoint or remove a majority of directors of the company, or
- where the company is under the control of another local authority controlled company.

Local authority influenced company and effective control
The 1995 Order enables a local authority to hold up to 50% of the voting rights of a local authority influenced company without bringing it into the public sector for finance and propriety control purposes. For a company to be deemed to be a local authority influenced company, the local authority will need to control 20 to 50 per cent of the voting rights in the company as well as have a business relationship with the company.

Voting relationship:
A Local authority influenced company as defined in the 1989 Act is one where:
- 20 to 50 per cent of the total voting rights of all the members having the right to vote at a general meeting of the company are held by councillors or local authority officers; or
- 20 to 50 per cent of the directors of the company are councillors or local authority officers; or
- 20 to 50 percent of the total voting rights at a meeting of the directors of the company are held by councillors or local authority officers.

Business relationship
In addition to having the above voting rights the local authority must have a business relationship with the company in order to be deemed to be a local authority influenced company. What constitutes a business relationship is specified in the 1989 Act and includes factors such as: local authority payments to the company accounting for 50 per cent or more of the company's turnover; local authority grants and ownership of shares and stocks in the company exceeding 50 per cent of the assets of the company; the local authority leasing or selling land to the company at less than best consideration.

The fact that a company is deemed to be a local authority influenced company does not, however, automatically make it a regulated company. The 1995 Order introduced the concept of 'effective control'. Provided the authority does not have what is called 'effective control' of the local authority influenced company, as specified in the 1995 Order, it will remain outside of the regulated category.

The key test is whether the local authority exercises dominant influence over the company or holds the right to do so. This means that a judgement on categorisation has to be made taking into account all the factors governing the relationship between a local authority and a company. The DoE Guidance of March 1995 suggests eight ways in which an authority could exercise 'effective control':

- holding rights to appoint or dismiss the majority of directors giving the authority effective control of the Board
- controlling pricing, investment or borrowing by the company
- managing the company's business or operations
- restricting the company's activities by placing non commercial conditions on any funding or limiting the company to trade solely with the local authority
- holding extensive reserve powers
- giving any general guarantee or indemnity in relation to potential liabilities or losses of the company
- holding an option to acquire a controlling interest in the company, or
- if there is evidence that the authority exercises effective control over the company by virtue of the spread of share ownership.

In practice it is very difficult to ascertain, at any given time, whether a company is or is not effectively controlled by a local authority.

The consolidated accounting test
The second test contained in the 1995 Order requires a local authority to hypothesise and consider, if it were a company registered under the Companies Act 1985, whether it would be required to prepare group accounts for the company in question. If the answer is 'yes', then the company would become regulated.

Unregulated companies
Private sector influenced companies that are 'effectively controlled' by the private sector escape being regulated. These are companies

where the local authority does not take an active part in the management and operations of the company. Therefore the local authority will not be obliged to treat the company as if it were part of the authority for capital finance and propriety purposes. Such companies include:

Local authority influenced companies that are private sector led
Local authority influenced companies that are 'effectively controlled' by the private sector as specified by the 1995 Order (see section on effective control above) are not regulated even if the local authority holds up to 50 per cent of the voting rights in the company.

Minority interest companies
Minority interest companies are companies where local authority associated persons (ie councillors and local authority officers) hold less than 20 per cent of the voting rights. They also include companies where associated persons hold 50 per cent or less of the voting rights but there is no 'business relationship' with a local authority.

Excluded companies
Some companies were excluded from the 1995 Order through a schedule to the order. These included public transport companies set up under the Transport Act 1985 and public airport companies set up under the Airports Act 1986. They are governed for capital finance purposes by their own, separate rules.

Companies may also be wholly or partially excluded from the regulatory regime through a direction of the Secretary of State (Section 68(1) and or 69(1) of the 1989 Act) excluding the company from coming within the influenced or controlled category. Local housing companies where the local authority has less than 50 per cent representation on the board have since been excluded from being influenced companies.

The controls imposed on regulated companies Financial controls
Capital finance transactions undertaken by regulated companies are treated as if they were undertaken by the council (Articles 12-17 of the 1995 Order) and are said to 'score' against the council's borrowing limit.

The council is obliged to provide credit cover for all capital finance transactions of the company including the receipt of capital receipts or notional capital receipts, receipt of European Union grants and credit transactions. In providing credit cover for such transactions the council is required to utilise some of its basic credit approval. This means that the council will have to forego borrowing to finance another capital project (see also page 40).

The propriety controls
These include various prohibitions such as the publication of party political material and the appointment of disqualified members as directors. There are duties placed on the company relating to the provision of information to members, the council and the councilís auditors; and on the disclosure of the council's interest in the company. There are also controls limiting directors' remuneration and expenses (Articles 4-10 of the 1995 Order).

Partnerships can be structured in a number of different ways ranging from informal joint meetings to formal legal structures such as companies with their own legal identity. There are key considerations for each option and the decision as to the choice of vehicle will very much depend on the local concerns and priorities identified by the council. Some of the factors that will influence the choice of vehicle include:

- the purpose for which the partnership is being formed
- the range of different interests that need to be involved in the partnership
- the level of community involvement that is being sought
- the role expected to be played by the private sector
- the degree of control expected to be exercised by the council
- the actual and perceived level of autonomy to be retained by the partnership
- the tax consequences for the local authority in setting up a particular partnership structure
- the cost of setting up and maintaining the chosen partnership vehicle.

This report focuses on the role and nature of the company model for undertaking partnership activities. However, apart from the company model there are various alternative structural options for partnership working. These are considered below.

Strategic alliances

Informal partnerships

Where a council simply wants to get individuals and organisations from across the sectors to discuss problems and solutions, in any area for which the local authority has responsibility, it can set up informal forums. Members of these forums have no authority to make decisions on behalf of the council. However, they can play a valuable consultative role in helping the council to take soundings directly from different sectors about issues of common interest or concern.

Councils have also established informal partnerships to bring together individuals and organisations to develop a vision, aims and objectives for the development of an area and to provide a vehicle that can co-ordinate joint advocacy or demonstrate to others that there is broad support for a range of objectives. The Greenwich Waterfront Development Partnership would be a good example.

Similarly many Single Regeneration Budget agencies have been informal partnerships rather than formal companies with the local authority or another public body acting as the accountable body.

Joint committees
Where two or more local authorities wish to undertake joint activities, they have the power under the Local Government Act 1972, section 101, to set up a joint committee. Joint committees are appropriate, where, for example, two or more local authorities decide to combine their resources to obtain economies of scale and greater commercial bargaining power. The Yorkshire Purchasing Organisation provides an example of a very successful local authority trading entity set up as a joint committee and formed to supply mail order products for educational establishments designated as 'public bodies' under the Local Authorities (Goods and Services) Act 1970.

Joint committees have also been used as a means of promoting the strategic objective of two or more councils. The London Housing Unit is an example of a joint committee set up and funded by most London Boroughs to provide information and advice on housing to those boroughs.

Joint committees have been used in two tier authorities to co-ordinate service planning and provision. The museum service in Norfolk is provided through a joint committee that brings together Norfolk County Council, Norwich City Council and the different district councils. The committee is responsible for establishing strategy, developing policy and delivering service.

Since joint committees have no independent legal status, one member of the joint committee will need to act as the lead borough and therefore has to take responsibility for the administration and other activities of the committee. In a relatively informal structure like this, when one member of the consortium decides to withdraw support it could cause a high level of destabilisation and disruption in the activity of the joint committee. Voting membership is also restricted to local authorities, although other members can be co-opted onto the committee.

Local Strategic Partnerships
A consultation paper on Local Strategic Partnerships (LSPs) was published by the DETR in October 2000 (DETR, October 2000). The aspiration behind LSPs is that all local public sector service providers should work with each other, the private sector and the broader local community to agree a holistic approach to solving problems with a common vision, agreed objectives, pooled expertise and agreed priorities for the allocation of resources. LSPs will also co-ordinate the efforts of existing local partnerships.

LSPs are intended to help local service providers co-ordinate their actions. But it is the individual partners who will remain responsible and accountable for decisions on their own services and the use of their own resources.

LSPs would be expected to include representatives from all the key public services such as health, police and probation service, all levels of education, Learning and Skills Councils, the Employment Service and benefits agency, local authorities and housing providers. LSPs will also need to ensure that community and voluntary organisations and the wider community as well as business representatives are involved in the multi-agency partnerships.

LSPs that meet certain minimum criteria will qualify for extra freedoms and flexibilities. For example, they will be able to modify government requirements in relation to the planning, accountability, monitoring and evaluation of various government sponsored initiatives as well as getting the Secretary of State to use the new power in the Local Government Act 2000 to amend or disapply certain legislative requirements if it will be for the well being of their locality.

Such LSPs will also be able to agree the allocation of the new Neighbourhood Renewal Fund targeted at the most deprived areas and approve the neighbourhood renewal plan.

Recognition of LSPs for these purposes will depend on partnerships demonstrating that they are effective, representative and capable of playing a key strategic role in the locality. Government Offices for the Regions will be responsible for advising Ministers on how far LSPs meet these criteria. It is envisaged that once partnerships have been recognised as the LSP for their area, they will automatically be deemed to have met any requirements for partnership working on subsequent government initiatives.

Partnerships required or encouraged by law

Crime and Disorder Act
The Crime and Disorder Act 1998 places joint responsibility on local authorities and police forces to work together and in partnership with other relevant agencies to develop strategies to reduce crime and disorder.

Health Act 2000
Since April 2000, under the Health Act 1999, it has been possible for health and local authorities to enter into closer partnership arrangements than was previously permitted by legislation. The government's view is that the new partnership arrangements will facilitate more 'seamless' services and will enable the needs of service users to be met in a more holistic way, irrespective of which is the originating provider of the services they receive.

There are three new types of arrangements which can be combined where appropriate. They are:

● Pooled budgets - enables money to be brought together in a discrete fund to pay for agreed services for a particular client group or groups. Funds 'lose their identity' for the purpose of service provision, but are still subject to best value regimes (in relation to local authority partners) and clinical governance requirements (in relation to health partners).

● Lead commissioning - one agency takes on the function of commissioning services which are delegated to it. Lead commissioning differs from joint commissioning in that authority is delegated to one partner in advance, instead of having to be negotiated along the way. The lead commissioner may contract with a range of providers, including those from the voluntary and private sectors.

● Integrated provision - this allows different professionals to work within one management structure. It is possible for one member of staff to perform several functions, with the aim of providing a 'seamless service'. Contracting with other providers, including the private sector, is permitted.

The arrangements cover a wide range of local authority functions, including social services, housing, transport, leisure and library services. For further information see *'Partnership arrangements under the Health Act 1999'*, DHN, 2000.

Not for profit organisations and those conducted for the benefit of the community

Charities
A charity is a body which is established exclusively for charitable purposes. The four principal categories of charity are:
1. trusts for the relief of poverty
2. trusts for advancement of education
3. trusts for the advancement of religion
4. trusts for other purposes beneficial to the community.

All these terms are defined in statute and/or case law. The concept of an educational charity is wide and extends to activities designed to develop character and personality (eg outward bound centres). Museums, art galleries and festivals, concert halls, theatres and libraries, provided they are for the benefit of the public generally, also fall within the education category. Several local authorities have set up charitable trusts under the education category to preserve certain historical buildings, wildlife sites or other areas of particular scientific or educational interest. An activity that is set up in the form of a charity can take the form of a trust or a company limited by guarantee.

The category of 'purposes beneficial to the community' provides wide scope for local authorities to provide services to the community through the use of a charitable institution.

Increasingly local authorities have been setting up bodies with charitable status to provide services that had previously been provided directly by the local authority, in areas such as housing, leisure and social services. These charitable or not-for-profit entities, although business like in their approach, are also regarded as being community orientated and generally more in keeping with the traditional values and objectives of local authorities than a company motivated by profit and returns to shareholders.

Charities enjoy substantial fiscal advantages in terms of corporation tax, inheritance tax and capital gains tax. They also enjoy a certain amount of relief from the national non-domestic rate. They are entitled to mandatory relief of 80 per cent and the local authority has discretion to give relief of the remaining 20 per cent where the ratepayer is a charity and the property is wholly used for charitable purposes.

The disadvantage is that the activities of the organisation must be strictly limited to those that are for charitable purposes. The process of gaining charitable status, although no longer as long and cumbersome as before, can still be a burden. Charities are under the regulation of the Charity Commissioners.

Trusts
Trusts (both charitable and non-charitable) have been used by local authorities in the past to pursue objectives beneficial to the

community. Trusts are normally property based and are created where property is either being held for particular purposes, or on behalf of others. Trusts may be charitable or non charitable.

A trust is an unincorporated body and does not create a separate legal entity. It is a collection of individuals drawn together to pursue a common purpose. As such, assets are legally owned by the trustees, and full personal liability rests with the trustees. Thus trustees are in a vulnerable position and may find themselves personally liable for the liabilities of the trust, even though they may not personally have committed any breach of duty or trust. Trusts are therefore generally used for operations where the financial risks are minimal.

Trustees usually need to operate by consent of all the parties. This means that they usually need a unanimous decision. Whilst having none of the advantages of incorporation, trusts and unincorporated associations are, however, free of the statutory restrictions, formality and requirements governing companies and their establishment.

Some trusts are set up for wholly charitable purposes and may be registered with the Charity Commission. Charitable trusts are not caught by the controls on capital spending contained in Part V of the 1989 Act (see page 55), although charities established through the medium of a company are brought within the Act's framework.

Trusts (charitable or non-charitable) can be used by local authorities as a way of co-ordinating the involvement of different organisations and individuals within the community. It may be an attractive vehicle for attracting grant funding from awarding agencies which prefer to fund partnership organisations.

Trusts have also been used by community based organisations to great effect. Development Trusts are community based organisations working for the sustainable regeneration of their area through a mixture of economic, environmental, cultural and social initiatives. They are independent, not-for-profit bodies, often registered as charities, which are committed to the involvement of local people.

Most are seeking to build an asset base and generate income, which will enable them to become financially independent and help them sustain their activities in the long term.

Companies limited by guarantee
This is a similar structure to a company limited by shares except that members do not own shares but guarantee a sum (usually nominal) on liquidation. Companies limited by guarantee are usually established for a not-for-profit purpose. The main purpose of the company will be geared toward the advancement or promotion of a charitable, social or other non-trading purpose. If the company makes 'profits' from its activities they are not distributed by way of dividend to shareholders as would generally be the case in a company limited by shares, but they are instead 'recycled' and used to further promote the company's objects.

The main advantage is to obtain limited liability and a separate legal entity (see page 19). A charitable company will have to be registered both with the Registrar of Companies under the Companies Act 1985 and with the Charity Commissioners. It will be subject both to company law and the regime of regulation of charities. Such a company will enjoy the fiscal advantages enjoyed by charities. However, companies limited by guarantee that are 'controlled' or 'influenced' by local authorities are will be caught by the rules on capital expenditure contained in Part V of the 1989 Act.

Local authorities have established companies limited by guarantee as joint venture vehicles to carry out activities which are beneficial to the local community, such as theatres, museums and entertainment centres or training and education facilities.

Companies limited by guarantee are also commonly used by community organisations. Working with Words Ltd is a company limited by guarantee with charitable status, providing opportunities for people with learning disabilities. It grew out of an advocacy project that was seeking to develop sign based software. Funding was secured through the European Union Horizon Programme to develop a communication and information service using symbol enhanced software based on signing language.

Industrial and Provident Societies and co-operatives
Industrial and Provident Societies (IPSs) are corporate bodies
registered under the Industrial & Provident Societies Acts 1965-78.
They are under the control of the Registrar of Friendly Societies and
as such not governed by mainstream company law or registered
under the Companies Acts. To qualify for registration a body must be
carrying on an industry, business or trade and it must either be a
'bona-fide co-operative' or a 'society for the benefit of the
community'. The requirement to be trading is not enforced in respect
of societies for the benefit of the community, though it is for co-
operatives (ICOM, 1997).

The characteristics of a co-operative include: only one vote per
member; a limit on the return on capital; if profits are to be
distributed amongst the members, this must be done equitably; no
artificial restrictions on membership.

The characteristics of a society for the benefit of the community are
similar to those of the co-operative, but profits and assets must not
be distributed amongst members and the society must be able to
show that 'it will benefit persons other than its own members'.

IPSs have similar structural flexibilities to registered companies. An
ISP can, unless its rules direct otherwise, hold, purchase, lease,
exchange or mortgage land. There is no difference between IPSs and
registered companies in terms of the liability of members and
directors since incorporation under the Industrial and Provident
Societies Act 1965 gives limited liability. An IPS cannot be registered
with the Charity Commission. If an IPS meets usual charity criteria -
and only a society for the benefit of the community will be able to
do this - it may apply to the Inland Revenue to be treated as a
charity for taxation purposes (ICOM, 1997).

IPSs encourage wide participation and accountability and the
involvement of the shareholders (who may be the employees and/or
members of the community and/or council members) in the

management of the operation. They are likely to have attractions for unions/staff due to the overlap of objectives with the local authority and the involvement of staff in decision making. Many housing associations have been set up as IPS. Some local authorities have set up IPSs to operate their leisure centres.

However, in spite of the purposes for which IPSs are established, where they are 'influenced' or 'controlled' by local authorities they are subject to the rules contained in Part V of the 1989 Act.

Greenwich Leisure Management Ltd is an IPS set up as a society for the benefit of the community. It was established as a response to spending cuts proposed by the council in 1992 which would have involved the closure of two or three leisure centres and the loss of up to 30 full time jobs. It was set up as an IPS with a Board of 11 elected workers, two elected customer representatives, three council representatives, one trade unionist and the managing director in an ex officio capacity. The council has no control over the leisure services but influence is retained through the council nominees on the board, via the annual grant and service level negotiations and via the lease on the buildings which remain in council ownership. This level of influence, however, leaves the company free of capital controls contained in Part V of the 1989 Act.

Other advantages of the company include: it can also apply for lottery and other funds as an independent organisation; it can be a private sector partner in SRB and other bids; it has fiscal advantages through getting rate relief and VAT relief; and it is a single purpose organisation which has empowered and enthused its workers through joint ownership (SEEDS, February 2000).

Greenwich Leisure Ltd has been able to develop a more entrepreneurial attitude through the empowerment of the workers and to expand with the growing leisure market. But its social and community objectives have remained fundamental and it continues to develop new initiatives (childcare for 28 part time women workers) and new partnerships (eg with schools and training providers).

Councils, like Harlow, have set up co-operative development agencies to support the creation and development of co-operatives. In Harlow an estimated 1500 people are involved in worker co-ops covering engineering, childcare, CD Rom development, catering, conservation, bus and taxi services and housing and property maintenance (SEEDS, February 2000).

Many of the successful initiatives have depended on support from the Co-operative Development Agency, together with the council and other partners, identifying a market opportunity and providing appropriate training to enable groups of unemployed local people to set up an enterprise to meet the identified need. Each co-operative has involved the establishment of a network of statutory agencies, trade unions, training providers, community groups and others who can support the co-op in some way. While most of the co-ops have required financial and management support in their early stages, they were all set up with clear business plans containing an exit strategy for external providers.

Partnership structures and arrangements with the private sector for commercial purposes

Contractual arrangements
The first question that needs to be asked, before setting up any new organisational structure is whether there is an actual need for a new structure. There are many situations where the objectives could be most simply met by a straightforward contractual arrangement whereby the council gets the job done through a contract or lease with another organisation. Contractual arrangements are best suited for projects involving a distinct client/contractor split of responsibilities, especially where the major share of the risk, the responsibility and the potential financial rewards for the project rest with the local authority.

The advantage of relying on contractual arrangements is that it avoids many of the difficulties and costs associated with setting up a company such as start-up and administration costs, conflicts of interest problems and the various other problems that are discussed in chapter 3 (see page 18).

Private Finance Initiative (PFI)

Despite numerous attempts, the use of PFI in local government was limited under the previous Conservative governments. Under the current Labour government the use of this approach has accelerated as local authorities have been guaranteed specific grant to meet the revenue costs associated with PFI schemes in the form of PFI credits.

PFI is a way of buying services that are capital intensive. Instead of the local authority financing a project by using borrowing approvals, the private sector finances the construction and then operates the services. In return the council will pay for the services over a period of years and these fees would include the costs associated with the capital investment (see page 42 for further information).

The main advantage for local authorities of PFI is that it enables capital projects to proceed that otherwise would not be possible as PFI projects do not require the use of credit approvals. Capital investment for PFI projects, unlike the case for conventionally procured schemes, do not score against the council's borrowing limits for capital spending.

The PFI credits that are available for meeting the revenue costs associated with PFI schemes are only available for certain PFI schemes that meet specific government set criteria. As councils become more confident the competition for the available credits will increase and presumably the prioritisation of projects will get progressively tougher. Schemes that do not require revenue support, such as those that councils can finance from their own resources or are self-financing, can go ahead without referral to government departments.

Although PFI is an option that increasing numbers of local authorities are considering when looking at how to meet their investment needs, the application of PFI in local government is still relatively recent. It continues to be controversial and concerns remain about democratic accountability and the impact on employees who provide the services. There is as yet no clear evidence about longer-term value for money. For a detailed discussion of the issues involved see *The Private Finance Initiative* by Janet Sillett (LGIU, 1999).

Joint venture companies
Joint venture companies (JVC) are another form of private/public partnership (PPP). They too are usually set up to deliver investment in services over a long-term contract. They are more likely to be adopted where the venture is expected to be free standing, deriving funding, assets and resources from the partners to the venture (as opposed to a central government source under PFI) and/or from other sources such as trading activities, charges for the use of assets or grant funding. They may be easier to set up than PFI arrangements and better suited for particular projects, such as those dealing with regeneration where a wide range of different interests need to be brought together. Each individual project will need to be carefully assessed to see whether PFI or a joint venture company would be the most suitable vehicle.

Development schemes
One important field of activity for local authorities and the private sector to combine their efforts has traditionally been joint ventures to develop land, buildings or communications within an area. There are many joint ventures that involve some form of leasing arrangement whereby the local authority leases land to a developer on terms which provide for sharing (through the rent payable) in the success of the enterprise. If the only connection between the private sector undertaker and the local authority in such situations is a lease or contract then it will avoid the problems associated with companies, such as being caught by the controls on capital finance imposed by Part V of the 1989 Act.

Companies limited by shares
The most common type of company is a private company limited by shares and incorporated under the Companies Act 1985. These organisations are, in law, separate legal entities owned by shareholders. They are generally managed on a day-to-day basis by directors appointed by the shareholders to take care of the business of the company. Such organisations are usually set up to trade with other entities in a competitive market environment and as such are open to risk. The main motive for companies limited by shares is the making of profit and ensuring returns to shareholders in the form of dividends.

The main advantage of a limited company is that the shareholders have limited liability. This means that they will not be liable for the debts of the company if the company makes losses over and above the amount which they have pledged the company to pay for their shares. Companies limited by shares have significant flexibility in terms of raising capital.

Companies limited by shares provide a useful vehicle for partnership because control can be shared through apportionment of company shares or directorships, according to the degree of involvement or control required. At the same time the constitution of the company could permit it to undertake projects which were beyond the legal capacity of local authorities.

However, a company limited by shares which is influenced and under the effective control of a local authority is regulated and subject to the capital control rules imposed on local authorities by the 1989 Act (see page 56 for explanation of the rules).

Local authority interest in limited companies may be for many different purposes. In some cases, legislation such as the Airports Act 1989, the Transport Act 1985 and the Environmental Protection Act 1990, has specifically required the setting up of companies for particular purposes, sometimes as a preliminary step along the road to eventual disposal or full-scale privatisation. In other cases local authorities have chosen to set up companies for different purposes.

The disadvantage of using companies relate to the loss of democratic accountability and other related issues discussed in chapter 3 (see pages 21-29). Actions undertaken through a company in which councillors or officers participate would be outside the normal range of controls designed to make their actions publicly accountable, such as answering to council meetings, the ombudsman's jurisdiction, the auditing process, and judicial review.

Another drawback of incorporation is the degree of formality which needs to be complied with under the Companies Act 1985. Obligations include the filing of accounts, annual returns, changes of directors and changes to the constitution of the company to the Registrar of companies on a regular and prompt basis.

Some local authority activities lend themselves more easily than others to being conducted through a trading company established for profit. These include services which derive income through charging users of the service such as car parks, markets, catering and restaurant facilities, IT, leisure and entertainment facilities. However, the powers of local authorities to trade commercially in competition with the private sector are limited to a relatively few instances set out in statute.

Wholesale privatisation of certain functions, through transferring undertakings to profit-making concerns has been carried out by some local authorities in particular service areas, such as care homes for the elderly where existing private sector healthcare operators are able to put forward competitive bids. But many local authorities seek to avoid disposing of their core service to companies limited by shares and established for profit. The preferred approach under these conditions is often to set up charities and other forms of 'not-for-profit' organisations (see page 61).

7 CONCLUSION AND RECOMMENDATIONS FOR CHANGING THE LEGAL AND FINANCIAL REGULATORY FRAMEWORKS

In deciding on the most appropriate structure to carry out a particular activity councils have a wide range of options to choose from, as described in the previous chapter. This report has focused on local authority involvement in companies in order to enable councils to develop a better understanding of the various complex issues involved in this particular model. While there are specific advantages to using companies there are also problems in using the company model for elected members, local governance and public accountability.

Good practice adopted by local authorities, as discussed in chapter 4, can go some way towards mitigating some of these problems. However, for those problems that stem directly from the legal and financial regulatory frameworks within which local authority companies are required to function, as discussed in chapter 6, more fundamental changes are required. Some of these changes are discussed below.

Relaxation of financial controls

● Introduction of the prudential framework

The government's Green Paper on Local Government Finance (DETR, September 2000) proposes the abolition of the current system of capital controls with a new prudential framework. Within this new framework, local authorities will decide the level of new borrowing that they want to undertake each year. However they will need to be able demonstrate that they are able to finance that borrowing and that they are complying with the appropriate professional codes of practice.

Initially the Government will impose restrictions on the rate of any increase in the level of local authority debt.

The ability to finance capital expenditure through borrowing will no longer be dependent on the level of credit approvals. Instead it will depend on:

- the rate at which the level of local authority debt is allowed to increase
- the requirements of the professional codes that form part of the self-regulatory framework
- the availability of the revenue streams to finance the borrowing.

The new prudential framework could assist local authority companies. For example, if a local authority controlled company that operates car parks wishes to install CCTV equipment to improve security, the debt charges and interest payments to repay the capital cost of installing CCTV can be financed either by the existing car parking charges or through higher car parking charges. Currently the capital expenditure on CCTV by the company counts as capital expenditure by the local authority and the council would have to utilise some of its basic credit approval and forego borrowing to finance another capital project. Under the prudential framework, it would be able to invest in CCTV financed through the revenue stream raised from existing (or higher) parking charges provided that:

- the level of increase in the local authority's debt does not exceed the statutory prudential indicators and
- the authority is able to satisfy the requirements of the relevant professional codes.

It is not clear yet how the prudential framework will apply to local authority controlled and influenced companies but it is possible that arrangements could be established in a way that enables these companies to finance investment through the revenue stream.

The draft guidance to the well-being power stated (DETR(a), December 2000, paragraph 42): 'Transactions by local authority companies would still need to be regulated under any new system of capital controls, since their expenditure has the same impact in the national accounts as that of authorities themselves. Nevertheless, the prudential system being proposed will increase the overall scope for local authorities to use their own resources to finance additional borrowing and therefore enhance local decision-making and accountability'.

The LGIU believes that the arrangements for local authority controlled or influenced companies need to be additional to those for the local authority itself. Otherwise the issue of 'capital displacement' will still arise.

Investment decisions made by local authority controlled and influenced companies need to be made on the basis of the business plans of those companies and the reasonableness of the assumptions that determine the ability of the company to finance the investment, through existing or new revenue streams.

● Repeal of Part V of the Local Government Act 1989

Part V of the 1989 Act imposes financial controls on certain types of local authority companies. Capital finance transactions undertaken by regulated companies are treated as if they were undertaken by the council and are said to 'score' against the council's borrowing limit (see page 55). The 1989 Act was introduced at a time when the primary objective of central government was to control and curtail the ability of local authorities to raise funds for capital expenditure. But it also has the effect of hindering partnership working with the private sector. The system of control is so draconian that it stifles local authority initiative and prevents the development of innovative and effective solutions to emerging problems that the government is keen to encourage.

The current method of controlling local authority companies under Part V of the 1989 Act is closely integrated with the overall capital finance structure. The changes proposed for this structure under the prudential framework (see above) mean that new arrangements for companies would be needed, which the government recognises (DETR, September 2000, Annex B, paragraph B10).

The LGIU believes that Part V of the 1989 Act should be repealed and replaced with a system of control that:
- allows local authority companies to use their own resources to finance additional borrowing, and
- treats them as separate from their parent local authorities.

Changes to company law

● Protecting council appointees who are directors from personal liability.

It is not clear at present whether local authorities have the power to grant indemnities against personal financial loss to their members and officers when they act as directors in companies that are established for a variety of different purposes. In order to put this issue beyond doubt, the government has promised to make an order under section 101 of the 2000 Act conferring power on local authorities to provide such indemnities. This would be welcome and should be done as soon as possible.

● Protecting the public interest within the company model

There is a need to investigate new ways in which public sector concerns can be addressed and the public interest protected within the company model. One possible way of doing this is through establishing a new type of company - the 'Community company' - as proposed in Butterworths (page D/320, paragraph 541) as an alternative and more radical approach to meet the requirements of local authorities acting with other organisations towards a common purpose. To encourage confidence in the use of this type of company as a legitimate partnership vehicle, a model constitution could be inserted into the Companies Act 1985 (Table A) setting out the various safeguards for local authority participation in such company.

It is suggested that the new Regional Development Agencies could perform a registration function for such community companies set up within a region by local authorities. These companies can be monitored and policed by RDAs working with regional chambers. Empowering legislation would make it clear that community companies are independent of the authority and that (in particular) the authority will not be responsible for the company's debts over and above any investment. This would give a clear message to third parties dealing with the company that the public sector, notwithstanding the authority's involvement, will not bale out the company in the event of insolvency.

Local authority trading

● 'Public bodies' for the purposes of the Local Authorities (Goods and Services) Act 1970

The powers of local authorities to trade with other local authorities and specified public bodies as well as their ability to receive payment for those goods and services are specified under the Local Authorities (Goods and Services) Act 1970. The government has set out its intention in the draft guidance to the well-being power published in December 2000 to review and consolidate the list of public bodies with whom local authorities are allowed to trade. It is important that this is done in order to remove uncertainty in this area.

This is important where a local authority is considering the establishment of a company for purposes of trading. Companies are not restricted in who they trade with. Clarifying the issue of who local authorities can trade with will provide councils with greater flexibility in deciding whether to act directly or through a company.

Conclusion

Even if all the above changes were made, it needs to be recognised that there will still remain a tension between the way a local authority as a democratically accountable, public sector organisation operates and the way a company operates. This will particularly be the case where local authorities participate in companies limited by shares as a means of working in partnership with the private sector for commercial purposes.

When a local authority seeks to carry out functions through the medium of a company issues such as: conflict between the interest of the local authority and the company; balance between public accountability and commercial confidentiality; and tension between protecting the terms and conditions of the workforce and maximising profit, will remain an inherent part of the arrangement. In many situations an IPS may be more appropriate.

Before going down the company route it is important to study the wide range of different structures available for local authorities acting on their own, or in partnership with other organisations. If, after doing this the company option is chosen, the particular problems associated with this model need to be scrutinised and steps taken to mitigate them as far as possible.

Some Examples of Companies

The following ten companies were used as case studies for the DETR study published in 1997. The information has not been updated since the original study and no doubt many changes have occurred within these companies in the intervening four years. None the less they provide a useful indication of the range of different purposes for which companies have been established and the various different ways in which they can be structured. A brief sketch of each is included here. For a full description of these companies see Local Authorities involvement in Companies: findings on research, DETR, November 1997.

Birmingham Technology Limited

This is a science park, started in 1983, with the aim of acting as an incubator unit for start-up or growing science and technology enterprises. It is a company limited by guarantee. The company is controlled by Birmingham City Council and hence is regulated. The board consists of 13 directors appointed as follows: 7 Birmingham City Council, 3 Lloyds Bank, 3 Aston University.

Reasons given for establishing the company:

- To increase economic activity - the company's primary aim has always been to stimulate economic activity in Birmingham.
- To introduce private sector management - the city council recognised that the skills required to develop this innovative concept were not available in-house (the objective of the science park is to act as an incubator unit for start-up or growing science and technology enterprises. The park is adjacent to the university and is designed to stimulate the roll-out of academic ideas into the commercial world).
- To work in partnership - it was recognised that success could only be achieved through a partnership approach involving the University and a financial institution.

Eurohub (Birmingham) Limited

Birmingham International Airport plc had been created to comply with Airports Act 1986 with shares wholly owned by the seven district councils of the West Midlands county area. When the opportunity arose in 1988 to develop, with British Airways, a second passenger terminal Birmingham International Airport decided to create Eurohub (Birmingham) Ltd as a joint venture company to design, build, finance and operate the new facility. This is because, as a local authority owned company, Birmingham International Airport plc was constrained in its ability to raise finance to construct the new terminal.

Eurohub is a commercial company which is designed to generate a return for its shareholders. It is a company limited by shares. It is a minority interest company for the local authorities involved and, hence, non-regulated.

Its board of directors are made up as follows:

3 Birmingham International Airport plc
2 British Airways plc
2 National Car Parks Ltd
1 District councils of the West Midlands
1 Forte (UK) Ltd
1 John Laing Holdings Ltd

Reasons given for establishing the company

- To obtain private sector funding - investment in the business was essential to maintain growth. Funding via LA sources was not available
- To increase economic development activity - the airport plays a key role in the region's development and stimulating its growth has a direct impact on the local economy
- Recognition of a commercial opportunity - the approach from British Airways was an essential part of the decision to pursue a joint venture approach.

Godiva Windows Limited

Coventry Contract Services, the city council's DLO, had been constructing plastic windows for the city council for over 10 years. Increasingly it was enjoying success in winning business to supply windows to other local authorities. Its internal market was reaching a natural end and its ability to serve potentially interested customers in a wider market was constrained by the LG(Goods and Services) Act 1970.

As a consequence the council advertised for a joint venture partner who would supply the authority with windows and take on existing staff in a genuine joint venture.

Godiva Windows was set up as a commercial venture with the objective of delivering returns to its shareholders including the city council. It was set up as a minority interest company for Coventry city council and hence is non regulated. Coventry city council owns 19.99% of the ordinary share capital with the remaining 80.01% being owned by Deceuninck UK Ltd

There are six directors on the board with one from Coventry City Council (head of Coventry Contract Services). The managing director was the former head of the window manufacturing plant at Coventry Contract Services.

Reasons given for establishing the company:

- To obtain private sector funding - investment in developing the business was necessary to maximise its potential
- To introduce private sector management - growing the business need different management skills, particularly in business development and marketing
- Recognition of a commercial opportunity - the DLO has already been successful in this business area. A joint venture was necessary to access wider public and private sector markets.
- Increase economic development activity - the DLO employed 22 people on this activity. The city council's aim was to retain this level of employment and potentially increase it as the company develops new markets
- To secure value for money - the competitive tendering of the

joint venture opportunity ensures that the price of windows to the authority was part of its evaluation.

Coventry and Warwickshire Partnership Limited (Aug 1994)

Coventry and Warwickshire Partnership was set up in 1994 following discussion amongst a range of public and private sector organisation in the sub-region about the most appropriate way of working together to deliver economic growth and prosperity. It is a company limited by guarantee. It is a minority interest company for the local authorities involved and, hence, non-regulated. Membership is open to organisations that share its goals with discounted rates for trade unions and appropriate 'umbrella' voluntary and community organisations.

The board of 26 directors is made up as follows: Private sector seven; local authorities five; TEC/Chamber of Commerce four; further education/higher education four; voluntary community sector three; trade unions two; and
Business Link one.

Reasons for establishing the company:

- creation of a forum to bring together three local authorities in the sub region (Coventry city council, Warwickshire county council, Nuneaton and Bedworth council)
- an opportunity to bring together a wide range of interests in pursuit of a common goal
- a structure for bidding for SRB and endorsing ERDF bids
- potential to create further joint ventures under a common umbrella.
- Presents private sector with an opportunity to directly influence strategy and policy across LA boundaries in the interests of a natural sub-region.

Kirklees Stadium Development Limited

The background to the formation of this company was as follows. The Huddersfield Town Association Football Club (HTAFC) needed £2.3m to bring its stadium up to minimum standard. But this was beyond the financial resources of the club. Also the Huddersfield

Rugby League Football Club (HRLFC) was ground sharing with HTAFC. The prospect for Kirklees MBC was that the town would lose both its football and rugby league clubs. All parties recognised that concerted collective action was required in order to resolve their individual difficulties.

Kirklees Stadium Development Limited was formed to plan, construct and build a new stadium which opened in August 1994. Primarily, the stadium is home to the local football club and rugby league club. However, from the start the stadium was envisaged to be multi-purpose in its use incorporating a number of commercial activities and has staged a number of musical and community events. (In addition, plans are being developed to develop the range of leisure activities undertaken on-site including a swimming pool, health and leisure club.)

It is a non-regulated company limited by shares. The issues share capital of £100 is wholly owned by the three partners: Kirklees MBC 40%, HTAFC 40% and HRLFC 20%. It has a board of six directors made up as follows: Kirklees MBC two; HTAFC two; and HRLFC two.

Reasons given for establishing the company:

● To secure private sector funding - the formation of a company in partnership with HTAFC and HRLFC gave greater credibility in raising the finance necessary to help build the stadium.
● To secure the involvement of private sector partners - the company provided a way of involving all three partie in an in dependent and meaningful way by which was not dominated by any one partner.
● Secured the continuation of professional football and rugby league in the town
● Provided a first-class multipurpose venue for regional, national and international sporting, commercial and other cultural events
● Contributed to the development of the Riverside Retail and Leisure Park and the improvement of former derelict land
● Create jobs during the construction of the stadium and in its ongoing operations

- Provided an opportunity to share in the profitable operation of the stadium
- Raised the profile of the Huddersfield/Kirklees area within the national press
- Accessed leverage and funds beyond the capability of each of the individual partners

Lancashire County Enterprises Ltd

Lancashire County Enterprises Ltd (LCEL) was formed in 1989 out of Lancashire Enterprises Ltd (LEL). The latter had been created in 1982 by the county council to provide a vehicle for progressing its economic development and training activities through an integrated approach.

In light of the legislative threats, enshrined in the LG&H Act 1989 which would have constrained LEL in its original remit, a major restructuring was undertaken in 1989 resulting in the formation of LCEL and Lancashire Enterprises plc (now Enterprise plc).

The principle objective of LCEL is to invest in Lancashire with a view to acting as a catalyst in promoting economic development in the county, to provide industrial premises and associated facilities for business, and to promote job creation and training, particularly associated with new technologies.

LCEL is a company limited by guarantee and is wholly owned by Lancashire CC. The Group structure includes six subsidiaries and three related companies. Preston Technology Management Centre (page 84) is one of the related companies.

The board of LCEL is made up of 19 directors as follows: 13 county councillors and the balance of six from private sector and other interests.

Originally funded by the county council by way of grants/loans under s137 of the LG Act 1972, the LCEL group of companies has been financially independent for its further development since 1989, relying on its resources and a combination of private sector borrowing obtained on the strength of its balance sheet and UK and European grants.

Reasons given for establishing the company

- Involve the private sector - in formulating their proposals, the CC recognised the essential need for effective private sector partnerships, particularly in securing the corporate investment aspirations of the initiative, which were beyond the resources of the authority to finance.

- The council saw the major benefits of using a company, as opposed to the authority, as confidentiality and the facility for speedy decision-making, both of which were regarded as essential in gaining the confidence of the business community.

- The choice of company structure provided a framework with which the private sector were familiar and which provided transparency and accountability in the company's operations.

- Provides focus for achieving specific objectives - LCEL is recognised by the private sector as the main focus and vehicle chosen by the CC for progressing its Economic Development and Training Initiative.

- The creation of subsidiary companies and related companies to pursue specific initiatives provides a focus for directors and management and, in turn, facilitate measurement of performance against identified objectives.

Preston Technology Management Centre

PMTC is a related company of Lancashire County Enterprises Ltd (LCEL), (page 83), and has the legal status of a company limited by guarantee. Established in 1993, its objective was to set up and manage a regional centre for the provision and promotion of technology.

The board is made up as follows: BAe one; Preston Borough council one; and LCEL three.

Reasons given for establishing the company

- Provides a framework for acting in a concerted way. The county council has a history of using company structures
- Traditional forms of private sector finance and support unlikely to be available and/or not suitable for such an innovative development (finance from charges to companies who occupy offices on site and who receive office services; constancy work and grant funding from the council and EU).
- Local authorities have a vested interest in the economic health of the local economy which the private sector does not necessarily have or to the same degree
- The provision of the company structure provides a sound basis for accountability and regularity.

Plymouth 2000 Partnership (SRB) Ltd

When the Plymouth 2000 Partnership successfully secured SRB funding it set up Plymouth 2000 Partnership (SRB) Ltd to deliver the SRB programme and any future allocations under the Challenge Fund. The company is limited by guarantee.

The 14 member board is made as follows: Plymouth City council five; Business community three; Community Development partnership three; Devon and Cornwall TEC one; English Partnerships one; Plymouth Development Corporation one.

The role of the board is to approve, manage and monitor the programme. In fulfilling this role the board is supported by a small executive team, comprising of the SRB manager and a small programme team.

The company has no employees. Management and financial services are provided by staff of the city council.

Reasons for establishing the company:

- A clear focus for the delivery of the SRB programme
- An organisational framework in which the public, voluntary and private sector can work together, one which is clearly independent of one constituent group

- A forum for airing and resolving different views
- Mechanism for ensuring accountability, regularity of reporting.
- Broaden the base of involvement
- Access to a wider skill base
- Mutual convergence of interest
- Builds credibility

Plymouth Marketing Bureau

The Marketing Bureau was formed in 1978 for the purpose of marketing the city as a tourist attraction. It has undergone restructuring in order to play a more strategic role in attracting domestic inward investment to the City and promoting interest in the city's commercial properties. Membership open to all local businesses. The Marketing Bureau is a company limited by guarantee.

The board is made up of 12 directors as follows: eight are nominated by private sector companies; and four by the council. The chair of the board is also the chair of the council's economic development committee.

The company has no employees. Management services are provided by the city council and professional counsellors.

SUBJECT AND REFERENCES LIST

'Power to promote or improve economic, social or environmental well-being: draft guidance to Local authorities', DETR(a), December 2000

'Power to promote or improve economic, social or environmental well-being: draft guidance to Local authorities', DETR(a), December 2000

'Quality and Choice: A decent home for all', DETR (b), December 2000

'Accountable partners? A councillors' guide to housing associations', Nigel Long, LGIU, 2001.

'Our towns and cities: the future. Delivering an urban renaissance', DETR, November 2000

Local authorities involvement in Companies: findings on research, DETR(a), November 1997.

'Power to promote or improve economic, social or environmental well-being: draft guidance to Local authorities', DETR (a), December 2000

'Power to promote or improve economic, social or environmental well-being: draft guidance to Local authorities', DETR (a), December 2000

'Local Authorities' involvement in Companies: findings on research, DETR(a), November 1997

Local authorities involvement in companies: good practice guide', DETR(b), November 1997.

'Power to promote or improve economic, social or environmental well-being: draft guidance to local authorities', DETR (a), December 2000.

'Local Strategic Partnerships, consultation document', DETR, October 2000.

Chapter 6
Different partnership structures   **57**

'Local Strategic Partnerships, consultation document', DETR, October 2000.

'Partnership arrangements under the Health Act 1999', DHN, 2000.

'An introduction to Industrial and Provident Societies', ICOM factsheet, Legal series No L.22, 1977.

'Seeds working papers on the social economy', SEEDS, February 2000.

'The Private Finance Initiative', by Janet Sillett, LGIU, 1999.

Chapter 7
Conclusion and recommendations for changing the legal and
financial regulatory frameworks

'Modernising Local Government Finance: a green paper', DETR, September 2000.

'Power to promote or improve economic, social or environmental well-being: draft guidance to Local authorities', DETR (a), December 2000

'Butterworths Local authority Companies and Partnerships', Robert Hann, first published 1997 and regularly updated.

Appendix   78

Local Authorities involvement in Companies: findings on research, DETR(a), November 1997.

Local Authorities and companies

by
Ramani Chelliah
LGIU

LOCAL GOVERNMENT INFORMATION

Acknowledgement

In writing this report I am indebted to the contributions made by my colleagues at the LGIU. In particular, the expertise of Hilary Kitchin, Pete Challis, Janet Sillett, Nigel Long and Ines Newman were invaluable in shaping the final form and content of this report. My thanks are also due to David Spencer and Jo Dungey.

Outside the LGIU, I am grateful to Stephen Sellers of Wragg and Co for his very useful and detailed comments. Thank you also to Clive Grace of Torfean Council for his positive support.